Marmalade Days

Marmalade Days by Linda Perry

Published by Poetry Space Ltd 2019

Copyright for all poems remains with Linda Perry's family.

Cover design Susan Jane Sims and Rosie Jackson using

'Birch Tor and Vitifer Mines' Monoprint by Anita Reynolds.

Editing: Rosie Jackson.

Typesetting: Susan Jane Sims.

All rights reserved.

No part of this book may be reproduced or transmitted in any form or by any means without written permission from the publisher.

Poetry Space Ltd Company Number 7144469

Reg.Office: 2 North St, Beaminster, Dorset DT8 3DZ

Printed and bound in Great Britain by Poetry Space Ltd.

www.poetryspace.co.uk

ISBN:978-1-909404-40-3

Marmalade Days

Linda Perry

For Fern

Foreword

Linda Perry's unexpected and untimely death in February 2019 left her family, friends and many who knew her in the Frome area, in huge shock. Linda had been central to the community in different ways for many years; her warmth, kindness and generosity of spirit were legendary.

Less well known was the fact that Linda was also a gifted poet. She'd always loved poetry and had written poems for many years, sharing some of them at Frome's popular Poetry Café. She attended workshops in the area – I first met her at my courses in the early 2000's – and she shared her passion for poems with friends. But it was in the last two or three years of her life that most of the work in this collection was produced, while she was coming to the monthly poetry workshops I held in my home in Trudoxhill.

I knew, of course, she had produced some powerful poems. But it was only in the shocked aftermath of her passing when, like many of her friends, I wondered how best to honour her, that I asked Linda's partner, Rob, for permission to put together a volume of Linda's work. And when he delivered to me a chaotic stash of papers, and I sorted through them, I finally realised the accumulated strength and beauty of what she'd been crafting.

For those who knew Linda, much of the content is not surprising: a deep love of people, family, and the natural world, a worried concern for the dire state of the planet, a commitment to green issues. But these are not heavy poems: they are playful, humorous, celebratory, witty, whimsical, showing a poet's pleasure and deftness with language. Linda was always willing to experiment with new forms: the poems here include anaphora (A Poem for the Sea); sestina (Snap Shots); mirror poem (Love Circles); ekphrasis (Why I Hate Millais); pantoum (Kelp Wears a Plastic Snorkel); eulogy (Enaudi, 'In Un Altra Vita'); sonnet (Gods of Stone) along with many open forms. But each one Linda made her own, and this collection shows the distinctness of her voice: lyrical, passionate, realistic, funny, practical, wise, compassionate.

The irony is that, if Linda were still with us, I doubt this volume would have come into being, at least in its present form. For she felt she was a poet still in the making, over-modest, quick to brush off praise. Yet the originality and variety of her work here do more than show her great promise, cut tragically short; they also reveal her already significant achievement. Linda was a woman so on the side of life, it is impossible to put her full legacy into words; but how wonderful to have her words too, as we have them in these poems, distinct, tender and original.

Rosie Jackson
Frome 2019

Contents

Benacre Broad, Suffolk	9
The Orchard Held in the Shed	11
He Made Everything	12
The New Pool	14
When	15
Over the Rim	16
A Poem for the Sea	17
Kelp Wears a Plastic Snorkel	18
Careless: An Anagram Poem	20
I See You and Am Afraid	21
Bold As Brass Buttons	22
Why I Hate Millais	24
Gods of Stone	25
Bradbury Rings	26
In Good Faith	28
Lost Sheep	30
Moss	31
Snap Shots: A Sestina	32
Midsummer Station	34
On Roofs of Russell St, Bath	35
Afternoon Mermaid	36
Song of Spells	37
No. 44	38
Moon	40

Wide Open…………………………………………….. 41

Pulling Apart……………………………………………. 42

River Walk ……………………………………………… 43

I Dream You Upstream ……………………………….. 45

Love Circles, A Mirror Poem …………………………. 46

On Arrival ………………………………………………. 48

Marmalade Days ………………………………………. 50

Einaudi, *'In Un Altra Vita'* ……………………………. 54

Benacre Broad, Suffolk

This is the beginning.
This uncertain division
where earth is not firm,
water is too thick
and sky does a double act.

Ditches and dykes flow, then stop.
This is where coots run, paddle
and dabchicks dabble,
reeds flourish purple spikes.

Below the marsh, below the silt,
invading armies lie lost deep down.
Axe, shield, sword all useless.

A band of reeds sighs a low requiem.
Last summer wooden ribs stood stark,
a prow appeared, then sank again.

Midges rise and fall above drowned bridges
and boats. Centuries-old marsh gas blooms
amongst marsh marigolds, golden docks,
sow thistles, water shrews.

Creeping from sludge under unthatched reeds
damsels and dragonflies dry their wings.
Bearded reedlings and Savi's warblers
scatter from the marsh harrier.

Water creeps, stills as though holding
a breath, then spills, sleight fingering
the banks, curls back into slate grey.

Foghorn boom of the bittern fills the air,
'Beware, beware the uncertain edges'.

The Orchard Held in the Shed

Eyes closed tight give me starbursts of light.
Eyes open, I see nothing.
No chink or slit, no ill-fitting plank
allows moon or starlight to filter in.

Cocooned in my sleeping bag, I lie
on the wooden floor, breathe in the rich, sweet air
and hear you wake beside me. The wooden walls,
roof, shelving, absorb sounds, release perfumes.

I stretch out, feel and pluck an apple from the shelf.
I know by the waxy skin, large bulbous shape,
sharp tang, it's a *Bramley's Seedling*.
Now you pass me one, smaller, dry to the touch,
a little lop-sided, an *Egremont Russet* or a *Nutmeg Pippin*.

Here in the dark, *Dabinette* conjures Grandma
with her fruit knife, lavender sheets, creamy rice pudding.
Autumn Pearmain, Grandad's favourite, is rough skinned,
smelling of earth, a little like him.

We play on, revisiting our childhood game,
identifying the orchard in the shed.
Tomorrow, in the harsh light, we'll wrap some
in newspaper, bring them to the old folks' home.

He Made Everything

He built a bed and a bedside table with a little lamp
and if you push a button the light comes on
but my dolly can't do that, so I do it for her.
He built a fort, a real one, with soldiers and horses
and a canon that really fires – matchsticks.
He built a car ferry, a real one,
so that when you wind a handle
the ramps go up and down
and the *Dinky* cars can drive on and off.
And he built an aerodrome
with all the runways painted
and enormous hangars for planes to taxi in and out
and a control tower with a proper aerial
made out of a paperclip.

To the left in wooden racks
chisels hang from narrow to broad, straight and curved,
each blade edge wrapped in oiled paper.
A grindstone and oilstone lie on the bench below.
Above the chisels, a line of pliers and pincers,
long-nosed, snub-nosed, goose-necked,
each one with a handle hooked over the rack
as if leaning a little drunkenly.
Above those again, the screwdrivers, sorted by type, length, width,
some of their handles bringing brash colour to the muted space.
To the right of the bench, claw hammers hook themselves up
and mallets, some leather-headed, huddle comfortably.
On the back wall a range of hacksaws, clamps and spanners,

shelves of white spirit, paints, glue,
Old Holborn tobacco tins full of nails and screws
nuts and bolts, washers and rivets.
Drawers of sandpaper, boxes of drill-bits, bags of rags;
and there, hunched over the workbench,
he measures, re-measures, marks the line,
tests the blade edge, lifts the mallet
and gently tap, tap, taps the chisel.
He settles into his rhythm, whistles softly to himself.
Amber curls drop to his feet from a horse's head
he carves for his granddaughter.
The air is rich with smells of apple, pine, walnut,
lingering linseed.

The New Pool

It stood, plastic blue, bulging in its metal frame.
The teacher stood, coated, muffled, back hunched to the wind.
We stood, purple-pimpled, nearly naked, scrawny knees knocking.
The school stood, proud of its purchase.

Half a mile away, the North Sea pounded the beach,
but here, Miss Catchpole tapped her clipboard.
'First three, in you go. Spread out along this end.'
Heads clamped in bathing caps, aliens breathing chlorine,
in we climbed. 'Don't stop,' she shouted. 'Don't put your feet down.'
Eyes stinging, turning was tricky, we bumped into the ends,
churned and choked, fought and floundered our way
through versions of breaststroke, crawl and doggy paddle
the whole seven lengths, the full fifty yards.

Later, the thick card, edged in blue, proclaimed the school,
the date, the distance and, on the dotted line
in beautiful copperplate handwriting – implying a dignity
and grace which had been sadly lacking – my name.

How proudly I stood, absurdly, ridiculously proud,
with my first certificate.

When

When I was six I packed my little suitcase
with Teddy, crayons, my ballet shoes,
a box of Newberry Fruits for Grandma.

When I was twelve I packed my red shoulder bag
with my favourite flares, T-shirt, pocket money, a toothbrush
and a map of Norwich because I planned to run away.

When I was eighteen I packed my rucksack with text books
on Virginia Woolf, education, sociology, a transistor radio
and an address for Halls of Residence.

When I was twenty-four I packed my lightweight holdall
with my TEFL certificate, bikini, flip-flops, passport
and a ticket to Ibiza.

When I was thirty I packed my overnight bag
with a nightdress, sponge bag, maternity pads
and new-born baby clothes for hospital.

When I was thirty-six she packed her little suitcase
with Teddy, favourite blanket, crayons, flags
for sandcastles, a box of chocolates for Granny.

Over The Rim

Great Gran used to read the leaves.
With milky eyes staring into the dregs
she witnessed accidents, wild storms,
a child lost.

World reporter and time-traveller,
peering over the rim, did she ever
foresee her own demise in the rise
of teabags which would deny her art?

A pot of tea draws us together,
soothes shattered nerves, mends friendships,
makes a perfect excuse for cakes,
'put-your-feet-up' breaks and biscuits.

But today it's a mug's game –
over a hundred and sixty million
bags a day in the UK.
Hidden in their neatly woven fabric
and crimped edges, nestle
plastic fibres, at least 20%.

Teabags have their dirty little secrets.
We're stirring up trouble.

A Poem for the Sea

A poem for the sea as it throws rocks in the face
of the wind and claws at the base of the cliffs.
A prayer for the sea at the mercy of magnetism,
moon-dragged east and west, gliding over and around lands,
filling and emptying rivers, basins. A song for the sirens,
for the inhabitants of the sea, silver-quick shoals of herring
hunted almost to extinction and for the fishermen too,
for soft beds of kelp, mermaids' purses, starfish and sea cucumbers.
A poem for long-distance swimmers, for whales, seals and eels,
for crawling crabs and lobsters, for the non-swimmers,
the limpets, cockles, goose barnacles, for waders, for paddlers.
A palette for the sea and its infinity, through turquoise,
samphire green, slate grey, burnt umber and aquamarine,
for white horses and midnight darkness. A prayer for traders
and trawlers, sailors and surfers, for foghorns, lifeboats
and buoys, and for conservationists, lobbyers, beach cleaners,
Greenpeace. A protest from the sea as it throws plastic
in the spume, drapes tar at the base of cliffs. A poem
for the life-blood, the sap, the well-spring of our world,
a plea to keep it clean. A poem for the seas of tranquillity and turmoil,
for the salt flats of The Wash, for Challenger Deep and Cape Horn,
for the careful gradations of rock, pebble, shingle,
for soft warm sand underfoot, for the surprise of a broken shell.

Kelp Wears a Plastic Snorkel

A collar of debris, a choker of waste
encircles our world, sails round our coast,
tangles with our feet. Kelp wears a plastic snorkel.
Barnacles cluster on a washed-up wine bottle. Look –

encircle the world, sail round our coast,
the sea's surface holds no tracks, no imprint of our passing, yet
barnacles cluster on a washed-up wine bottle. Look -
it carries a scrap of paper, a message.

The sea's surface holds no tracks, no imprints of our passing, yet
borne on the waves, words unfurl in our fingers.
A scrap of paper carries a message
PLEASE HELP! SAVE ME!

Borne on the waves, words unfurl in our fingers
and a child's drawing of a starfish, a whale.
PLEASE HELP! SAVE ME!
A shrill cry, a demand, a prayer from the deep.

A child's drawing of a starfish, a whale
fills front pages, is on prime time TV.
A shrill cry, a demand, a prayer from the deep.
'Toothbrushes, Lighters, Found in Neptune's Locks.'

Filling front pages, on prime time TV:
'Fishing Tackle Wraps Up Skeins of Seaweed,
Toothbrushes, Lighters Found in Neptune's Locks.'
When will we stop this tide of pollution?

Fishing tackle wraps up skeins of seaweed,
tangles with our feet. Kelp wears a plastic snorkel.
When will we stop this tide of pollution,
this collar of debris, this choker of waste?

Careless: An Anagram Poem

When did we begin to *care*
so little for our vast rich *seas*,
our fertile green *acres*?
Who started the wholesale *sale*
of our resources, fixed the *scales*
over our eyes, made the *race*
for profits so *crass*?
What fool would not *see*
how this unfettered greed of more for *less*
would cause such damage to the frail *lace*,
the web of life, and break its bonds, its *seals*?
Why do we stand by, close our *ears*,
deny the dangers, pretend we're in the *clear*?
How did we become so arrogant, so *careless*?

I See You and Am Afraid

I see you come through the gate, cross the courtyard,
walk onto the lawn as though you owned the place.
Your rufous chest ripples in bronze and gold
like molten armour, catches the sunlight.
Black chevrons chequer your wings, and your tail's
a mastery of design and balance. There's a crisp white ruff
about your slender neck, your cheeks are brightly rouged
and backed with emerald; all is crowned royally purple.

You strut your stuff past the winter honeysuckle,
stop to inspect the late roses and parade up and down
the rows of leeks. Today you have an entourage bobbing
and curtseying in your wake: drab browns pecking and scurrying,
currying favour with your highness. Yet, for all your imperial ways,
there is a fragility, a delicacy to your legs, a sinuous softness.
Vulnerable, you process, bejewelled and beautifully plump,
an exotic come to brighten our grey days.

Then, over the hedges comes a *crack crack, pop pop*. And I am afraid.
Alert to assassins, you throw your head back in alarm,
cry warnings, *kertuck kertuck,* and rocket skywards –
straight into the firing squad. Now you will be hung till the blood
drips from your fine head, your entrails will be drawn
and you will be roasted in the fires till the fat runs
from your beautiful breast and you are reduced
to a mouthful or two. For 'tis the Jolly Boxing Day Shoot.

Bold As Brass Buttons

We have a history spanning five thousand years
from found, curved shells and polished stones
to hand-carved wood and bones.
More items of adornment than functional when
we clung to chests of Chinese Emperors and Pharaohs.
Long ago, in the hands of artists,
craftsmen created our exquisite forms,
(it's true, a lucky few are still worked with care).
Once seen as useful, our influence spread.
Everyone took to us, the world was ours.
Bold as brass we marched with armies,
all sides believed well-polished buttons won a war.
We've held men's bulging ardour in check,
contained heaving bosoms, expanding bellies,
been torn off in passion and despair,
snaked down a queen's spine,
lined up in a wedding gown.
There's a seam of violence running through our story.
We've been hammered, beaten, punched, struck.
Today, oil is extruded from the earth, refined,
heated, cooled, laid in polymer sheets and
we are stamped out in our millions.
Imagine all the shirts, skirts, trousers and blouses,
coats and cloaks, the pyjamas and nightgowns.
Yes, we have eased our way into your beds,
your work, your play, your pubs and clubs.
We have witnessed snatched kisses,

overheard secrets, truths and lies.
We're all over your lives.
We've even given you a belly button.
We are ubiquitous, inconsequential,
unnoticed, until one of us goes missing.
We work quietly and well, individually or together.
In single file or two abreast we are the best.
We are not intrinsically racist or sexist,
religious or secular, nor political,
though some have tried to make us so.
From collars to cuffs, from rough tweeds
to widows' weeds, whether in silk, wool,
glass, pewter, brass or gold, we hold
the fabric of the world together.
We are infinitely adaptable and ready to step back
from our present, plastic manifestation –
we've heard it's ruining the world.
Our white-collared button cousin in The White House
says there's a battle going on as to 'who has the biggest…'
so one of us might blow it all.

Why I Hate Millais

after John Everett Millais' 'Ophelia', 1851-2

It was him, Millais, who perpetuated that first lie
for eternity – the picture Gertrude wove in a few lines,
the lie she gave life to on my death. Gertrude,
queen of survival in a man's world.

Imagine the scene. Remember I'm supposed to be mad.
Was it a) me lying face down in ugly sluggish water
with flies around, or b) me beautiful, at rest, at peace,
floating down a river? You think she told the truth?
Why would she make a horror harder to bear?
But *I* know. I was there, with mud stopping my mouth,
lungs awash, ditch water sloshing in and out of my eyes,
my ears. Oh, I don't blame her, Gertrude - in her own way
she was perhaps trying to be kind, to Hamlet.
But him, Millais, he took that little lie and fixated on it,
spent months, *months*, in a spot in a field by a river
and painted. Was he the one who was mad?
For Christ's sake, he had a girl lie in a bath of water
for weeks. Of course she got ill. Of course he was mad.
I should know.

There are people who think I should be flattered, grateful –
after all, I'm now and forever a thing of beauty,
not a bloated corpse – but it's the damage he's done to suicides
that makes me loathe him. It's the covering up, the layer upon layer,
the hiding, the glossing over. Millais, a brilliant artist?
Oh yes. A product of his age? Oh yes. Brilliant and mad?
Oh yes. I know.

Gods of Stone

I met a traveller by some poor waste land
who swore about the giant quarry stones
that filled the gateway and had therefore banned
him access to this brambled site, where bones
of crows, long-dead elms and broken trucks
bleach, rot and rust, to fungi and to dust.
'The bastards, they've got a nerve to fence this
corner, call it a conservation site.
We were in tree houses, the front-line fight
to save the woods from being blown to bits.
Now look into the abyss: the savage scar.
They're screwing the place, hour, by hour, by hour.'
He pissed on their sign, brushed tears from his eyes,
spat on gods of stone, raised fists to the skies.

Badbury Rings

after 'Like That Only' by Imtiaz Dharker

We've parked the car and read the signs
which insist we REMOVE ALL VALUABLES,
CHECK IT'S LOCKED, and, at the gate,
THIEVES OPERATE.

We're sure we did, but just in case
we retrace, test the doors, peer in,
scan the floors for valuables,
spot dry mud, pens, toffee wrappers.

Turning, I wonder who ate them?
A blur hurtles down the hill
and, still at breakneck speed,
charges through the gate.

An angry bull stops in front of us, heaving,
red in the face. 'It's a disgrace,' he bellows,
'people… people like you…', then runs out
of breath; a small crowd gathers and holds theirs.

'That's my car, you…you…,' he tries again,
and I worry about the strain on his heart,
think to say, 'Calm down,' but instead turn
to check on our Astra,

only to find two identical silver-grey,
sixteen-hundred, hatchback saloons
sitting side by side, haloed in sunlight,
confusing immaculate twins.

We too, now red, offer sincere apologies,
a bottle of water, say we ought to have noticed
the likeness. Calmer, he accepts the peace offering,
drinks, and comes up gurgling with laughter.

Like a Mexican wave, shoulders relax
around the crowd, normal breathing resumes
and chatting, sharing stories of confusions
grants one another absolution.

A hush falls as we climb, following
the track sculpted way back
over two thousand years ago,
adding our footfall, keeping the ancient way fresh.

On top of Badbury Rings, someone says
'Long ago, they herded their animals
up here for safe-keeping.'
Astra Man offers us a toffee.

In Good Faith

There's a section along Church Road
where ash and beech grow thick each side
and intertwining arms meet overhead
creating a green nave. Sunrise
splashes in from the eastern, altar, end.
Back when elms grew there as well,
Mr Abel, the organist, would ride
the mile to church and home again
three times each Sunday on his sturdy steed,
a three-speed bike, well oiled.
Silent as a moth he flew along Church Road
in a dark tweed suit, sporting
two pairs of white bicycle clips,
one worn conventionally, the other
wrapped around the jacket's wrists.
To stop the draughts of course.
His bike light, a faint glimmer,
barely reached the tarmac.
No matter, you could say,
the bike and Mr Abel knew the way.
After the accident we mumbled prayers
for him in church, which must have worked,
because the very next week he was back
in the organ loft. The morning coffee ladies
had a whip round, presented him
with good advice, new lights
and a Day-Glo vest

which were never seen again.
But he did take to singing
Guide Me, O Thou Great Redeemer
on his way home in the dark –
and that worked too.

Lost Sheep

Wind-strimmed gorse scours the path,
scratches my shins. I lost the signed way
a mile ago in the valley and now I find
rabbit tracks offer to take me everywhere.

I choose ways up. Grassy clearings grant
cool relief for my legs. I pull my soft socks high,
push along sharp-edged tunnels.

Quickening sloes dust the hillsides.
Virginal white blossom laces harsh thorns.

Ahead, the crest is topped with rocks.
Ribs, skull and thigh bones on the outcrop
have taken on the tones of age-old stone.

Moss

Moss drapes cellular blankets
over yew needles
knitted together.

Snap Shots: A Sestina

Suddenly, it seems, the season is turning.
Seeking the sun, pale shoots and limbs appear,
unfurling leaves, hitching up skirts. The park
gathers people like a street band playing
at carnival, or a blockbuster film.
Preparations made, sunhats dusted off,

blankets chequer the grass and kids tear off,
throttling back past dogs, picnics, turning
into robots, tigers, supermen, film
heroes. Hungry, thirsty they re-appear,
refuel, run, until at last playing
for time, they're tortoises leaving the park.

From office block windows and full car parks,
dazzling suns multiply, bounce off
and back across the streets, hunting, playing
into musty yards; dank corners turning
a little drier. Barbecues appear,
men in aprons, dishes wrapped in cling film.

Mates bring beer. The 'Chef' wipes away a film
of sweat from his brow. His Jurassic Park
apron looks tired, but more friends appear,
more beer, and the afternoon wobbles off
into evening. Night, the fire out, turning
for bed, he finds his kids still up, playing.

Old bones shuffle out, sit and doze, playing
dead, marking time, while rewinding the film
of their lives, remembering, returning
to the young, pain-free days when they too could park
their bottoms on the grass, yet be off
in an instant. Tears hover, smiles appear.

Girls in trainers, strappy tops, don't appear
to notice staring eyes. Headphones playing
they jog past traffic jams, bus queues, sprint off
down alleys, vault low walls, tangle with a film
crew shooting celebrities in the park,
laugh while the cameras keep turning.

Midsummer Station

A rabbit hops across the line.
Butterflies sip at sweet-smelling buddleia.
In the light breeze a Kit-Kat wrapper skips
across the platform and lands neatly by the litter bin.
A long, long way away a siren sounds and,
in the roof struts, a pigeon coo woos softly.
The announcement system hisses, sighs, crackles, dies.
Dust stirs, but we settle deeper into the afternoon.
The train is late. Even the clock has stopped, waiting.

On Roofs of Russell Street, Bath
after Douglas Dunn's 'On Roofs of Terry Street'

Redundant chimneys stand shoulder to shoulder,
shudder for warmth on chill March nights.

Lame pigeons build apologies for nests,
decorate soot-stained parapets white.

A buddleia has taken to the sky,
roots in a blocked gutter, finds earth, air, water.

In summer, purple blooms wave above double deckers,
entice high-flying Admirals to drink.

Afternoon Mermaid

Cast adrift this lazy afternoon
from ties of work and home
and all that anchors my life,

I walk the chalk downland way.
Ripe fields ripple the horizon.
A stand of beech breaks the waves

and I swim through the sea of corn,
legs hidden in thigh-high harvest –
a mermaid in a golden ocean.

Song of Spells

Her songs are spun from the sweep of swallowtails,
from the seeds of thistledown,
spun from our smiles and our shame,
spun from the secrets of sticklebacks
swimming the shallows.

She sits beside the stream and sings spells
that shake the seasons,
spells that stretch space-time,
shift our sense of self.

Sizzling summer slaps snowflakes into sandcastles.
Societies suffer shocks as centuries are shuffled slapdash.
We seek sanctuary.

She scores her spells into song-sheets,
sampled, scratched onto discs,
but scarcely sought after, seldom sold.

No. 44

I positioned this chair carefully.
From here there is only moonlight,
the table, one bottle, one glass,
an oasis of monochrome.

Full bright moonshine soaks through
the threadbare curtains,
floods the kitchen table.
I trace the long shadow
cast by an empty wine bottle,
which points to the door like a sign.
Drained after hours of work, and the wine,
I slump in my seat,
feet heavy, reluctant to move.

Behind me and on both sides
his life spews from boxes, cases,
cupboards, shelves, trunks, sacks,
cereal packs, cracked cups,
loo-rolls, records, tools, toasters,
postcards, lampshades, tins of pilchards.
Sheets and sheets of music
cascade across the floor.

I concentrate on this small space
it took all day to create.
Somewhere in this house
there's a piano my brother used to play.

I haven't found it yet,
but Beethoven's *Moonlight Sonata*
seems to drift through the window.

Moon

Moon settles herself on the couch, shakes out her silver cloak.
It cascades over armchairs, ripples up roller blinds,
shimmies across the floor to the door
where the draught excluder keeps it captive.
'I can't stay long,
I have an important job to do.'
'Then why did you come?' I ask.
'Curiosity, I suppose, and to put Sunny Boy's nose out of joint.
He'll be jealous; he can't get close to anyone.'
Moon yawns and stretches - a silver cat in a silver sea.
'It never stops, dragging the oceans round and round.
Yes, there is magnetism, but it's mind over matter too
and if I lose concentration for just a moment, it's chaos.
Ships run aground, babies are conceived.'
Next door, at number 24, Lucy studies the cycles,
notes days, dates, temperatures,
records them in a little red book, believes the figures,
surmises tonight's the night for safe sex,
looks forward to Jamie's return.
She can't see who is lingering at number 26.

Wide Open

Throwing the door wide open, you dance into the living room,
squeeze me speechless in a tight bear-hug,
toss your shoulder bag to the floor and fling yourself
onto the settee. 'Surprise!' Mischievous eyes
scan the room, 'So what's new?'
And I can't think of a single word, except, 'You.'

You, who left a year ago wearing heavy hoodies
over angry shirts, vests like chain mail
covering a skin too thin.
You, who left with a rucksack full of safety plasters,
sterilisers, cure-all pills, spare socks, spare hats,
spare this, spare thats. 'I need to cope if I'm stuck
on my own in the middle of nowhere. I might need a rope!
I need to get away. I have to go.' 'Where?'
'Oh anywhere, I don't know.'

You, who left, back bent, shoulders bowed, scared,
scowling through the goodbyes,
have shed the hoodies, the chain mail vests,
the rucksack full of insecurities,
and sprawl here wearing confidence and smiles.
So when you ask, 'What's new?'
I say 'You.'

Pulling Apart

Lost in this full-blown summer's day,
we're not used to being like this.
Gently touching one another
with careful words, hugs too intense,
we pull apart.
Talking of this and that,
the heat,
the journeys that brought us together,
love, regrets, times lost, laughter, the years gone by.
We wrap each other in memories
while our late friend fills the chapel.

While our late friend fills the chapel
we wrap each other in memories,
love, regrets, times, lost laughter, the years gone; by
the journeys that brought us together,
the heat.
Talking of this and that,
we pull apart
with careful words. Hugs too intense.
Gently touching one another,
we're not used to being like this.
Lost in this full-blown summer's day.

River Walk

When we got out of the car, I saw him, over by the dyke, slate grey against the reeds, motionless, waiting. The sun wasn't exactly shining, but there was a brightness, a lightness about the sky. The cool offshore breeze ruffled our hair and tugged the surface of the river into wavelets. We wrapped ourselves in hats and scarves and I shouldered the backpack. If you'd been sitting on the bench, you would have seen us, my brother, arms linked with Mum up ahead, me dawdling a bit with Dad. From the lifeboat shed where we'd parked, it's about a mile due west to the footbridge, the rutted track following the river's curve. We had given ourselves plenty of time. It was another two hours before high water, before we needed to be at the bridge and so, as planned, we ambled slowly along through the tar-black ramshackle shacks with their colourful litter of fishing floats and buoys, where you still see gnarled fingers deftly mending nets.

    Old George was there that day and, seeing us, paused from sorting the fish to touch his cap in acknowledgement, scaly fingers leaving a silver splash on the filthy rim. Days gone and Dad would have stopped to yarn, but that day we passed by silently, past the low slim canoe club shed and past the ranks of dinghies, bare-masted, bows pointing up stiffly like a regiment on parade saluting the Captain, my dad. Past the riverside café, where Dad always stopped for coffee and a custard tart, past Sid the chandlers, where Dad would tap the barometer and Sid's wooden leg, reckoning you needed both to get a true forecast. Past the Harbour Inn with its wavy-line sign, well above our heads, showing the 1953 water level when the east coast flooded. The Harbour Inn where he took me on my 18th birthday and encouraged me to try every one of the local beers, sure I would like one. I didn't!

    From the pub it's a single file footpath along the top of the bank to the bridge. On the left, the water surges and swirls past boats and jetties, the incoming tide overriding the river, flooding the mud-flats for miles inland; acres of safe haven for wading birds, providing perfect conditions for beds of samphire and sea lavender. To the right, pastures are edged by ditches and dykes rather than hedges. There, cows graze among swans and low mists roll the seasons over. There, we would gather mushrooms by the bucketful and cook them in the tiny galley on our boat. Abandoned landing stages lean drunkenly and brazen seagulls fattened on day-trippers' chips squat the rocks where we used to go crabbing. Seaweed, marsh gas, fungus, the smells of a heaven.

    From 15 stone, Dad had lost a lot of weight, reduced to a few pounds of ash, but he weighed heavy in my backpack, on my shoulder, in my heart. My feet dragged along the sandy path. I caught up with Mum and my brother and we stepped onto the bridge together, hands held. With a lifetime to talk about, we had nothing to say. There are never enough words and words are never enough, but we gazed over the miles of water and meadow, the unchanging vastness changed hourly by the rise and fall of the tides. We emptied the ash and watched as it settled on the river, then, pulled and tugged by the swirls and eddies, it dispersed. We waited. The heron flew down and settled, slate grey, motionless.

I Dream You Upstream

I dream you upstream
past the sail-less windmill,
staithes and withies,
past inseparable swans,
seasonal geese and eel nets.

You weave through reed beds,
ride the tide high,
then comes slack water
and you leave part of yourself there
amongst the waders and empty shells.

Slow at first, you meander back,
track through rushes,
then gather pace,
join the main race
and stream fast.

You have gone –
but I feel we're close
when I come here
to this bridge
over this river.

Love Circles (A Mirror Poem)

She kept them all
in ribbon-tied bundles
smelling faintly of roses
in a small cardboard suitcase
at the bottom of the wardrobe:
fifty-nine Valentines.
Tender, humorous, romantic
some bought in Woolworths, some handmade,
some hand-delivered, some stamped abroad.
Impish cupids from Karachi,
love darts from Darwin, hugging hearts from Hong Kong,
crimson capitals LOVE from New York City.
On shore-leave, he must have scoured the shops.
Far out in the ocean, sitting on his bunk,
he worked from a set of watercolours,
kiss-licking the end of his paintbrush,
'Always yours, always.'
She was his lode star.
Love circled the world
again and again.

Again and again
love circled the world.
She was his lode star.
'Always yours, always.'
Kiss-licking the end of his paintbrush,
he worked from a set of watercolours,
sitting on his bunk, far out in the ocean.
On shore-leave, he must have scoured the shops:
crimson capitals LOVE from New York City,
hugging hearts from Hong Kong, love darts from Darwin,
impish cupids from Karachi.
Some stamped abroad, some hand-delivered;
some handmade, some bought in Woolworths.
Tender, humorous, romantic,
fifty nine Valentines
at the bottom of the wardrobe
in a small cardboard suitcase,
smelling faintly of roses,
in ribbon-tied bundles.
She kept them all.

On Arrival

The evening takes on a neat air
after the flutter of questions and filling in of papers.
The room is trying to look comfortable.
We settle in. You on the bed sometimes,
sometimes practising yoga, pacing, a little
ungainly dragging the drip trolley.
Night is the nurse keeping vigil
and you in your bed, hooked onto monitors.
She sits in her tidy blue uniform,
eyes on the screen, ears tuned to the beeps,
diligently handwriting, recording vital signs
even though a print-out zigzags silently onto the tray below.
Night is the nurse quietly taking your temperature,
blood pressure, pulse, time and time and time again.
You, my child, restless, unbearably uncomfortable.

The dawn is late.

At eight you're five centimetres dilated.
There's a change of shift, energy.
Morning is crowded with noise, jostling uniforms
reading the notes, the monitors, you.
Long ago you let go of the birthing pool
and now I see you have left the room.
You're a surfer, way out at sea studying the swell,
feeling the lift, riding the wave; sometimes.
Sometimes churned under thundering white water,
you're left clutching at the mask. There's no time to recover,

no time and the whole room is willing you to push, push, push,
keep going, keep going, keep going
and I want to scream, 'Can't you see? She is.'
Desperate, I stand on the shore holding your hand,
but you are so very far away.

There is silence.

Suddenly you're back, surging with life,
and here, in this 21st century hospital,
the semi-circle of women around your feet
channel their energy with you,
eyes ablaze with intention, faces taut with effort,
they urge you, guide you, call your name,
catch your daughter as she slithers into this world
and, laughing, crying, put her to your heart, your breast.

Child of my child.

Marmalade Days

A shaft of light from the open back door cuts the dark
of a winter evening and shows us down concrete steps to the path.
My brother and I hurry behind Mum, her slender figure there
to guard us against ghoulies and ghosties. We swing the lobster pot
between us, a deep, willow shopping basket, hard, with sharp edges
where pieces have broken off. It scratches our legs if we don't co-operate.
Tonight we let it bump on the ground so Mum won't hear.
Mum loves the lobster pot.

And there's the lorry, at the end of the path. A hurricane lamp swings
under a green awning where dancing shadows climb the soft walls.
This open-backed canvas cave smells of earth, of damp tents
and boat covers. On tiered, wooden shelves are stacked boxes
of sandy carrots and enormous swedes. Cauliflowers burst
from nests of dark leaves, onions glitter in brittle skins.
Sacks of potatoes hunch together, parsnips rub shoulders,
bunched beetroot blush.

Fearless in the soft lamplight we hop up and down
to get a better view. Mum reads out from her list. Old Mr Samson
jumps onto the back of the lorry. To us he is one hundred years old
but he grins as he moves among his groceries. Like a dancer
he balances, reaching everywhere. We hold our breath,
wanting, not wanting, yes, wanting him to topple, just once.
He winks. He reads our thoughts. His gnarled, work-worn fingers
delicately lift sprouts, leeks and turnips for our pot.

It's not just produce from his market garden he brings
once a week, but bread, tea, sugar, tinned pilchards,
corned beef, *Camp Coffee* and cakes, delicious cakes.
The lobster pot is filling fast but Mum's still singing
through her list. Tired now, we sidle round
and move to the back of the lorry. By climbing
on the huge rear bumper we can poke our heads up
into this wonderful treasure-tent on wheels.

A sharp, mouth-watering smell of oranges fills my nose.
I see Mr Samson pass a whole boxful to Mum. A boxful,
what is going on? I know, aged eight, that we only ever buy
four oranges a week. Like bananas, they're a luxury.
We always share these fruits and never have a whole one,
unless we're ill. Apples we can help ourselves to, apples from the shed.
Tonight we're told to carry the orange box between us to the kitchen.
Careful, mind and come straight back.

We creep along the path with our precious cargo. As we open
the back door, light strikes the fruit, turns them into glowing globes,
pulsing suns. I rub one between my hands, transfer
the exotic perfume to my skin, feel its bumpy waxiness.
So many oranges, one each at least for school tomorrow.
We run back. Mum has her purse out now and we climb up
for one final look at a tray of sugary doughnuts, iced buns,
oozing custard slices and lurid jam tarts.

Mr Samson is talking to us. Are we going to help Mum,
will we be good? We answer *yes*. He nods, puts a sticky bun
into a paper bag, and with *Mind you share,* he hands it to us.
A box of oranges *and* a bun, we carry the lobster pot with extra care.
That night, I drift off to sleep with a bittersweet tang
still on my fingers. Next morning we ask for an orange, for school.
Mum laughs, tells us they're *Sevilles*. Who is *Seville* and why do we
have *her* oranges we wonder, as we head off.

Running home up the lane into a knifing east wind,
I taste something in the air, a prickling sharpness
that explodes as we open the back door. Our kitchen
is a witch's cavern, full of billowing steam.
A rolling boil inside the vast jam pan throws out citrus clouds.
Mum scoops up golden lava with the old proverb jug.
Red-faced, she fills the too-hot-to-handle jars, places them
in rows by the open window to set.

Shreds of peel hang in the liquid sunshine, suspended like insects
caught in amber. Mum seals them with waxed discs.
A saucer's daubed with puckered pools. We sit on the back step,
suck blobs of marmalade from sticky fingers. Heaven.
Mum made sixty pounds of marmalade each winter, enough
for one jar a week (for family breakfasts), a few extra for presents.
Years passed. We graduated from box-carrying to label sticking;
from shredding peel to, finally, filling jars for Mum.

Of course, later each year there was jam making,
then jellies, chutneys and pickles, but we loved
the marmalade making best. It was as if the sun dropped
into our kitchen and lit up those cold, dark January days.
So today, here on holiday, when I see among the postcards
of venerable saints, white-washed villages, feisty flamenco dancers,
this one card, filled with oranges, I know it's the one for you
and that on the back I will write, *Marmalade Days.*

Einaudi, 'In Un Altra Vita'

The sun slips above the horizon, burns the reed heads gold.
Fire floods across the beds, licks away the pre-dawn cold,
gilds iron-mud salt-flats and steely ditch-water.

Puddles are burnished into bronze shields, and a heron
is crowned king. Oystercatchers pipe in the day, dunlins
dance across the wet sand, create intricate etchings.

The sun, brighter, whiter now, drains the heavy gold
from the scene and, as though released from a Midas touch,
reeds sway with the incoming breeze, the tide.

I squat motionless on the bank watching the heron, stock-still,
the two of us immobile in an ever-changing world.
This is land reclaimed from the sea.

I can hear the water watching, waiting its chance.
The heron stands large in his landscape, but his
spindle-thin legs bother me, too slender to tether him.

As if on cue, he cracks open giant wings and, with laboured
nonchalance, beats away to another realm, leaving me on this bank,
on this path, where I come to feel at home, but am lost.

Standing now, I'm the high point in these low lands,
where earth and water are ever shape-shifting,
where the edge is always difficult, always blurring.

Later, I will go to your funeral and hear Einaudi's
'In *Un Altra Vita*' playing. From cafés, bars, concerts,
radio stations, it will bring me here again and again –

to the edge, where you flew away.

Acknowledgements

Thank you to Linda's family, Rob, Demelza and Orion, for encouraging this project even in the midst of their grief.

Thanks to Mandy Griffiths, one of Linda's closest friends and poetry mates, and to the members of the Trudoxhill poetry group who helped bring these poems into being: Brenda Bannister, Gill Harry, Jane Hughes, Chris MacFarlane, Nicholas Mann, Wendy Perry, Ann Phillips, Pete Woodcock, especially to Jane, Chris and Wendy for their help with typing.

Thanks to Rose Flint and Helen Moore for their endorsements and Susan Sims at Poetry Space for her immediate enthusiasm in taking on this publication. Devon artist Anita Reynolds very generously gave permission to use her beautiful monoprint *'Birch Tor and Vitifer Mines'* on the cover.

www.anitareynolds.com

Thank you to everyone in the Frome area who loved Linda and helped us feel this book would be welcome.

LINDA PERRY spent her childhood on the Suffolk coast before moving to Bath for teacher training. From the early 80s until her death in 2019, she lived with her partner and children in Frome, where her work in the wholefood shop and with green issues made her a vital and much loved part of the community.